J·O·S·E
CANSECO

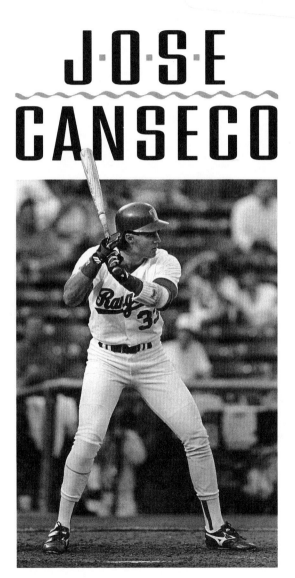

J·O·S·E CANSECO

Baseball's 40-40 Man

Nathan Aaseng

Lerner Publications Company ▪ Minneapolis

This book is available in two editions:
Library binding by Lerner Publications Company
Soft cover by First Avenue Editions
241 First Avenue North
Minneapolis, Minnesota 55401

To Grant and Clark Olsen

LIBRARY OF CONGRESS CATALOGING-IN-PUBLICATION DATA

Aaseng, Nathan.
  Jose Canseco : baseball's 40-40 man / Nathan Aaseng.
    p.   cm. — (The Achievers)
  Summary: A biography emphasizing the career of the star
outfielder of the Oakland Athletics.
  ISBN 0-8225-0493-6 (lib. bdg.)
  ISBN 0-8225-9586-9 (pbk.)
  1. Canseco, Jose, 1964-   — Juvenile literature.
2. Baseball players — United States — Biography — Juvenile
literature. 3. Oakland Athletics (Baseball team) — Juvenile
literature. [1. Canseco, Jose, 1964-   . 2. Baseball players.
3. Oakland Athletics (Baseball team) 4. Cuban Americans
— Biography.] I. Title. II. Series.
GV865.C313A18   1989
796.357'092'4 — dc19
[B]
[92]   89-2279
                                                                    CIP
                                                                     AC

Manufactured in the United States of America

ISBN 0-8225-0493-6 (lib. bdg.)
ISBN 0-8225-9586-9 (pbk.)
Library of Congress Catalog Card Number: 89-2279

6   7   8   9   10   98   97   96   95   94   93

Contents

1

Too Good to Believe?

It was one man against thousands on a cold autumn night at Boston's Fenway Park. Those are intimidating odds for anyone—unless the man is Jose Canseco.

Canseco (Con-SAY-co) had just upset the faithful followers of the Boston Red Sox in the first game of the American League Championship Series by blasting a home run. Now the fans were determined to get back at him, to rattle his concentration in any way they could. There would be no escape for the Oakland A's slugger when he jogged to his position in right field. In the cozy surroundings of the major leagues' smallest ballpark, Canseco would be closer to the hostile fans than to any of his teammates.

The fans had come prepared with the perfect heckling ammunition. A widely read baseball writer had recently claimed that Canseco's muscular body had been built by using drugs called steroids.

The writer had also said that other ball players sometimes referred to steroids as "Jose Canseco milkshakes." The use of steroids is neither illegal nor against baseball's rules, but it is unsportsmanlike and can produce dangerous side effects like liver damage and mental depression.

The accusation had upset Canseco, and he had denied the charges. He was insulted that people thought his strength and skill in baseball were the results of taking drugs rather than the results of all the hard work he had put into making himself a bigger, better ball player.

What better way to get under Canseco's skin than to bring up this sore spot! As the Oakland right fielder jogged to his position, a sing-song chant went up around him. "STER-OIDS!" "STER-OIDS!"

Canseco heard what the fans were chanting. For a moment he looked around at the jeering crowd. But instead of lashing out at them or pretending to ignore them, he smiled. Then he began posing for them, flexing his muscles.

When asked about it later, Canseco refused to fault the fans. "They didn't start the steroid rumors," he shrugged. "They were having fun and so was I. This is too big a show to get uptight."

The next night the fans tried a new angle on the same theme. "JUST SAY NO!" they yelled. Canseco responded by tipping his hat to them, and by later hitting a two-run home run to tie the game. Canseco's homer turned the game around and dimmed the Red Sox's pennant hopes.

Canseco had his best year in 1988, but late in the season he was dogged by rumors that he had used steroids.

Known for his tape-measure home runs, Canseco surprised the
baseball world by stealing 40 bases in a season.

This incident provides a key to understanding Jose Canseco, both his personality and his accomplishments. Canseco is an easygoing man who is comfortable with himself. He tries not to take himself, his occupation, or his fame too seriously. At a young age he discovered the secret of patience. In a business where emotions often run wild, he understands the need to control himself so he can get the most out of his ability.

The taunts of the fans were also an unwitting tribute to his tremendous achievements in sport. Sadly, this is an age in which people no longer simply sit back and marvel at the astounding performances of top athletes. Widespread cheating and drug use, especially use of steroids, have made doubters out of fans. They keep asking themselves whether it was ability and hard work that made the sprinter or weight lifter set a new record or whether it was something artificial. Could anyone possibly have accomplished the things Jose Canseco has without taking steroids?

Jose Canseco is so big, so strong, and so awesome a hitter that he can hardly help but attract the disbelief of fans and the accusations of hostile critics. The steroid rumors are a sign that the Oakland star is almost too good to believe.

Canseco did not always seem to realize how special a ball player he had become. In spring training before the 1988 season, he had set his goals for the season.

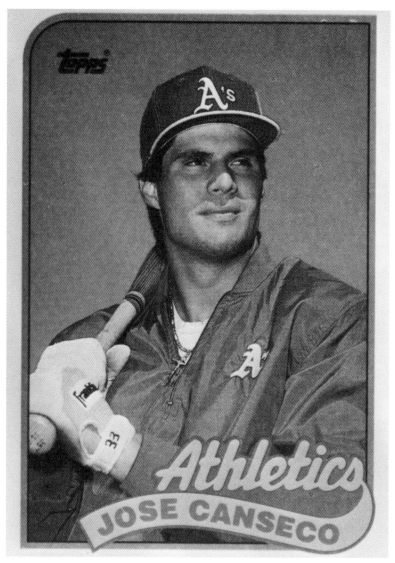

Canseco baseball cards have become a treasured commodity for card traders across the country.

Then he told reporters that he was aiming to hit 40 home runs and steal 40 bases in 1988. At the time, Canseco knew those were impressive goals, and he figured that probably no more than half a dozen players had ever accomplished such a feat. But they seemed reasonable goals to him and he did not expect much of a reaction to them from the baseball world.

The fact was that no one in the history of professional baseball had ever hit 40 home runs and stolen 40 bases in the same year! Canseco was stunned when he found out what he had announced. Had he really been so brash as to claim he could do something that had never been done? His statement had gotten plenty of attention in the media, especially since Canseco had stolen just 15 bases in each of his first two full seasons in the major leagues. Canseco worried that he might end up looking like a conceited fool when he failed to reach such a lofty goal.

Once the surprise had worn off, though, Canseco realized he had not been brash. He knew better than anyone else what he could do on the baseball field. He was certain that his 40-40 vision was not just a mirage. So what if no one else had ever done it? Canseco believed that it was within his reach, if only he worked hard enough.

Canseco played third base in high school.

14

2

The Road to the Major Leagues

Because of his Hispanic name, Canseco was frequently interviewed by reporters who seemed to expect him to speak English poorly or speak only Spanish. Although he was born in Havana, Cuba, Canseco has lived nearly all his life in the United States. His father, Jose Sr., had taught English at a college in Cuba. Jose Sr. and his wife, Barbara, had wanted to leave Cuba ever since the communist government of Fidel Castro had taken over the country in 1959.

The spring of 1965 was hardly a convenient time for them to make the move. In addition to their young daughter, Teresa, the Cansecos had to care for twin baby boys, Jose and Osvaldo (Ozzie). The twins were born on July 2, 1964. When the boys were nine months old, the Cansecos had a chance to leave Cuba. They took it and settled in Opa-Locka, northwest of Miami.

Jose Sr. eventually obtained a job as a territorial manager for an oil company and, in 1975, moved the family to southwest Miami. There, the Cansecos lived among Miami's large Cuban community.

As boys, Jose Jr. and Ozzie looked so much alike that few people could tell them apart. Their father kept them straight by remembering that Jose is slightly taller and has a birthmark on his right hand.

The Canseco twins enjoyed playing baseball. Like many boys, they dreamed of one day playing in the major leagues. Such a hope may have seemed more real to them than to many others, though, because they had a live example in their neighborhood. One of their baseball teammates was Burt Pascual, the son of Camilo Pascual. Pascual, a Cuban pitcher, played for 18 years in the major leagues.

Neither Jose nor Ozzie offered early hints of the powerful build that would be the Canseco trademark. The twins were actually two of the thinner players on their Coral Park High School baseball team. Jose, standing about 6 feet, 1 inch, weighed only 155 pounds when he started high school. He played third base while Ozzie pitched and played in the outfield.

It was Ozzie who seemed to have a flair for the game. Scouts from several major league teams kept track of his progress. By the end of his senior year, though, Jose had begun to catch up. He had grown a couple more inches, put on an extra 15 pounds, and

Jose (back row, fourth from right) and Ozzie Canseco (back row, fifth from right) were two of the premier players for Coral Park High School in Miami during their senior year.

was hitting the ball with authority. But even with his .400 batting average and frequent home runs, only one major league scout was interested in him. By coincidence, the Oakland Athletics' scout for the Miami area happened to be the retired pitcher, Camilo Pascual! Pascual urged his club to grab Jose in one of the first rounds of the 1982 free-agent draft. During the draft, teams divide young, unsigned players among themselves. Teams with the worst won-lost records are allowed to choose players first.

None of the A's took Pascual's suggestion about Canseco seriously. On draft day, in June 1982, Ozzie was claimed as a pitcher in the second round by the New York Yankees. (Since then, he has continued to play professional baseball, but has not enjoyed the success his brother has.) Meanwhile, Jose sat through round after round, waiting for his name to be called. Pascual had been unable to convince the A's management.

In a desperate attempt to get the A's to draft Canseco before another team did, Pascual threw his wallet on the table and offered to pay for Canseco's signing bonus. Finally, in the 15th round of the draft, Oakland went along with the scout and selected Jose.

In his first days as a professional player, Jose did little to reward Pascual's faith in him. In six games with Miami of the Florida State League, Canseco collected only one hit, a single, in nine trips to the plate.

Before long, the A's sent him across the country to Idaho Falls of the Class A Pioneer League. There he managed to put up some respectable numbers. In 28 games as a part-time player, Canseco batted .263 with two home runs. It was at Idaho Falls that the Oakland organization decided that this tall athlete might not have the quick reactions required to play third base. They experimented with him in the outfield, where he could put his running speed to better use.

Canseco's batting suffered during his first couple of years in the minor leagues, but he began to work harder.

The next season the A's sent Jose to Madison, Wisconsin, of the Class A Midwest League. While he began to settle into his position as an outfielder, he had trouble in the batter's box. Canseco struggled through 34 games with a .159 average and three home runs. Finishing the year at Oakland's Class A club in Medford, Oregon, he regained enough of his confidence to hit .269 with 11 home runs. Along with that, though, came the humiliation of trudging back to the bench after striking out in more than a third of his chances.

Canseco says he was unfairly called lazy during his first few years in the minor leagues. Part of the problem was that his stride is deceptively smooth. Even when he is running as fast as he can, he does not seem to be putting forth much effort.

Also, Canseco experienced the usual problems that face 18-year-olds in baseball's farm systems. Far from his familiar Miami surroundings, he barely had time to get comfortable in one place before he was assigned to a different team. He was further shaken when his mother died in the spring of 1984, and he missed six weeks of the baseball season.

Later that year, Jose began to realize how much work it would take to become a major-leaguer. He took to the weight room with a vengeance. His developing power boosted his home run total to 15 that year, while his average climbed to .276 for Oakland's Class A Modesto, California, club.

While those were better-than-average statistics, Canseco knew they were not enough. Those were the kind of numbers you could expect from a 15th-round draft choice playing in the low minor leagues. But 15th-round draft choices are not expected to be more than fringe major league players at best. Canseco wanted to be better than that. He realized that he would need a big year if he wanted the Oakland coaches to take him seriously.

When Jose Canseco moved up to Class AA in the spring of 1985, he reported for duty with Oakland's Huntsville, Alabama, team. He was a pumped-up version of the 175-pound infielder who had first signed with Oakland. The hits and home runs came so suddenly that he could hardly believe the results himself. One night in particular had him amazed. In that game, Jose had five hits in five at bats (including three home runs) and drove in nine runs!

In 58 games with Huntsville, the now 220-pound Canseco slugged 25 home runs, drove in 80 runs, and batted .318. Those numbers sparked the interest of Oakland officials, who rushed him up to the A's top farm club in Tacoma, Washington. Even after he left Huntsville, Canseco was still one of the main topics of conversation there. Despite playing less than half a season at Huntsville, he was named the Southern League's Most Valuable Player for the year.

The streak did not stop when he reached Class AAA Tacoma, either. Although his home run frenzy tapered off to 11 in 60 games, Canseco batted .348 and drove in 47 runs for the Pacific Coast League team. Continuing his rush up the minor league ladder, Canseco was called up for a brief tryout with the major league club at the end of the year. Canseco had gone from a Class A team to the major leagues in one calendar year!

The 21-year-old was so excited at getting to bat in

his first major league game that his knees were shaking. During his tryout, pitchers took advantage of his nervousness. They frequently baited him into lunging after breaking pitches, and they struck him out 14 times in his first 20 plate appearances.

Realizing that his lifetime dream was turning into a nightmare, Canseco stepped up his concentration. He began to wait for the breaking balls to break. Instead of trying to pull outside pitches into left field, he slapped them to right. Once pitchers found they could no longer get him to go after the outside pitches, they were forced to throw closer to the plate. In his September stay with Oakland, Canseco batted .302 and clubbed five home runs, including one that soared over the left-field roof of Chicago's Comiskey Park. Fewer than 30 players had accomplished that feat. He struck out a third of the time, but, with his huge swing, even his misses could be unnerving to a pitcher.

When Jose's 1985 totals from Huntsville, Tacoma, and Oakland were added up, record keepers discovered that Canseco had unexpectedly put himself on a collision course with success. Altogether he had batted .328, hit 41 home runs, driven in 140 runs, and become the 1985 Minor League Player of the Year.

3

King of Batting Practice

Canseco was excited about attending the A's spring training camp in 1986, but he had little chance to enjoy the novelty of the experience. From the time he arrived, he was targeted by the press as baseball's next superstar. National magazines ran feature stories on him in which they raved about his ability and proclaimed him to be the best new player to come along in years. Reports from the Athletics' training camp in Phoenix talked of a 6-foot, 3-inch, 230-pound giant who seemed intent on launching a baseball into orbit. Oakland batting instructor Bob Watson paid him a huge compliment by calling him a combination of Roberto Clemente, Dale Murphy, and Reggie Jackson—three of the best hitters ever to play the game.

Canseco's blasts were measured against the most legendary long shots of history.

Early in his rookie year, Canseco was already being compared to one of baseball's best hitters, Reggie Jackson (above).

For example, the Phoenix stadium measures 430 feet to the center-field fence, which is reinforced by a 45-foot-high wall. Many players had hit one ball over the wall, but no one had ever done it twice. Not only did Canseco blast a pitch over that wall, he blasted many balls over the wall during batting practice.

"I'm just a rookie. I'm still learning," Canseco protested, bewildered by all the media attention. Among the things he needed was more experience on defense. Because Oakland coaches needed Canseco's bat in the lineup but wanted him to sharpen his skills as a fielder, they put him in left field, the least demanding outfield position. There, Canseco could develop his skills without the pressure of a long throw from right field to third base.

It was difficult for Canseco to concentrate on his job when crowds of reporters followed him everywhere, distracting him and wearing him down with interviews. The situation got worse when word of his batting practices leaked out. By the second month of the season, Canseco was receiving more attention for what he did *before* the games than for what he did *during* the games.

The sight of Canseco stepping into the batting cage and pummeling pitch after pitch into the far bleachers or onto the sidewalk beyond the ballpark practically hypnotized onlookers.

"When Jose goes up there, everything stops," former Oakland manager Jackie Moore said, "because everyone wants to watch."

One baseball writer claimed that Canseco had turned batting practice into an art form. Reporters for various media around the country urged fans to go to the ballpark early when the A's came to town. Canseco's batting practice show by itself was worth the price of admission, they said. Oakland's opponents, even the most seasoned veterans, were awed by Canseco's power.

During batting drills before a game with the New York Yankees, Canseco stopped his bat in midswing (an action known as a "checked swing"). The ball struck the bat anyway. Despite Canseco's effort to stop, there was still enough force in his halfswing to send the ball over the right-field fence. "I'm not watching this anymore," declared Yankee third baseman Mike Pagliarulo, a power hitter in his own right. "He checked his swing and hit one of the longest shots I've seen." Yankee manager Lou Piniella talked about pulling his pitchers off the field during Canseco's batting practice because he was afraid the machine-gun barrage of homers would make them nervous.

Not all of Canseco's fireworks were launched before the game. He started the 1986 season just as he had left off in 1985. Several months into the season he was leading the major leagues in runs batted in (RBI).

Canseco's rookie card, issued by Donruss, is rapidly gaining value among baseball card traders.

He also was battling for the lead in home runs. It was one of his singles, however, that had the Baltimore Orioles wondering if he was human.

Canseco hit a drive that bounced off the left-field wall at Baltimore's Memorial Stadium. The ball was hit so hard that it rebounded halfway to the infield before the speedy Canseco could make it to second base! He had to stay at first. It may have been the hardest-hit single in baseball history.

Gradually, though, Canseco's production began to slip. Experienced pitchers shrugged off the fearsome appearance of the slugger's muscles and mighty swing. Such power did not mean a thing if the batter could not hit the ball. Realizing that the rookie was an impatient, aggressive hitter, they began to tease him with pitches that faded just out of his reach. Canseco began overswinging, and he nose-dived into a slump.

Batting instructor Bob Watson blamed the batting practice circus for Canseco's slump. He believed that Canseco had gotten caught up in trying to please the fans with 500-foot clouts rather than practicing his hitting form. Not only was he not doing the drills he was supposed to be doing, but he was picking up some bad habits.

Meanwhile, Canseco's relationship with the press was falling apart. The 21-year-old's shyness and nervousness were misunderstood. Reporters criticized him for being moody and uncooperative. Canseco began to dislike the press for having built him up to be "some kind of monster robot." It was a critical time for Jose Canseco.

The Oakland ball club did its part by limiting media interviews with their young star. Some of the pressure was further eased when California Angels rookie Wally Joyner started to outshine Canseco. Joyner became the rookie to watch, especially after fans voted him to start for the American League All-Star Team.

Joyner was the first rookie from either league to start in an All-Star game. Canseco was also named to the American League All-Star Team, although he didn't get a chance to play.

Even though some of Canseco's pressures were eliminated, it was still up to him to continue batting with confidence. The key was to stay in control of himself. Instead of angrily defending himself against Watson's claim that he was showing off in batting practice, Canseco admitted that it was true. "A lot of times, I'll catch myself trying to impress the crowd," he said. While it might have been fun to keep enjoying the gasps of onlookers, Canseco realized he had to look to the future. His first job as a young player was to learn, to practice, and to improve.

Canseco also showed a veteran's wisdom in dealing with his problems at the plate. Rather than getting overly concerned about the slump and worrying that he had lost his skill, Canseco gave the pitchers some credit. "You have to expect that the pitchers will make their pitches now and then and get you out." He continued to believe that if he worked hard in practice and did not panic, his natural ability would resurface and he would start hitting again.

Canseco had many discouraging moments throughout his rookie season. He struck out 175 times and his batting average for the year was a less-than-dazzling .240.

But he battled through such frustrations to deliver some big hits at important moments. Canseco hit 33 home runs and had 117 RBI, one short of the Oakland club single-season record of 118 runs batted in. Fourteen of his hits were game winners for a team that won only 76 games that season.

Canseco's contributions were recognized in the balloting for American League Rookie of the Year. Wally Joyner had enjoyed a sparkling first year with a .290 average, 22 home runs, and 100 RBI. Pete Incaviglia of the Texas Rangers had belted 30 home runs. Yet Canseco was named the league's top rookie. Incaviglia's performance might have won the award in most years. But, matched against Canseco, the Ranger outfielder did not receive a single first-place vote.

During 1987 fans and the press again swarmed around Oakland's powerful young home run leader. Baseball experts were checking their record books to see how this intimidating newcomer might compare

to the most fearsome sluggers of all time. That season, though, Jose Canseco did not mind all the attention. That was because the popular young slugger who was drawing the crowds in 1987 was not Canseco, but rookie Mark McGwire!

While the 6-foot, 5-inch McGwire chased the major league record for most home runs by a rookie, Canseco slipped into a supporting role. Canseco was able to concentrate on improving his game.

Gradually he learned to be patient and to fight the urge to swing at pitches that were off the plate. He learned to shorten his swing and protect the plate when the pitcher had two strikes on him.

At the same time, Canseco recognized that hitting is only part of the game. He refused to settle for being a designated hitter, a role he was assigned 30 times during 1987. He wanted to play a bigger part in the game. As he gained experience playing in the outfield, he became a more skilled defensive player. In fact, Oakland switched him from left field to right field to take advantage of his strong throwing arm.

Canseco's improvement came slowly but steadily. Lost amid the fanfare of McGwire's record-breaking 49 home runs in a rookie season, it was barely noticeable. But even though Canseco's home run total dropped from 33 to 31, he was becoming a more complete player. He improved his batting average 17 points, to .257, and reduced his strikeouts to 157.

Mark McGwire (right) helped to take some of the pressure off Canseco (left) in 1987. McGwire set a record for most home runs by a rookie.

While McGwire received most of the acclaim, it was Canseco who again provided the most key hits. Seventeen times in the 81 games the A's won, he came through with the game-winning hit.

4

The 40-40 Season

During spring training of 1988, Canseco mulled over goals to set for himself during the year. In the previous season, Eric Davis of the Cincinnati Reds had tried, unsuccessfully, to combine 40 home runs with 40 stolen bases. It was this milestone, combining the very different talents of speed and power, that stirred Canseco's imagination. He announced that he wanted to hit 40 home runs and steal 40 bases in 1988.

Although he certainly did not intend it that way, Canseco could not have found a better way to grab the spotlight away from McGwire. For one thing, unknown to Canseco, no major league player had ever hit 40 home runs and stolen 40 bases in the same year. In 1973 San Francisco Giants outfielder Bobby Bonds had come the closest. He stole 43 bases that year and hit his 39th home run with nearly a month to go.

Bobby Bonds (left) was one home run short of a 40-40 season with the San Francisco Giants in 1973. Eric Davis (right) had 37 home runs and 50 stolen bases in 1987. It was Davis' attempt to break into the 40-40 Club that had Canseco thinking of it when spring training began in 1988.

But he struggled through the final 21 games of the season without hitting that last home run.

It also seemed a tall order for Canseco to clout 40 home runs playing in Oakland. Because the nighttime wind at the Oakland Coliseum usually blows toward home plate, even well-hit baseballs do not travel far there.

Canseco's bold challenge seemed even more brash when baseball fans examined his stolen base record. Jose had stolen only 31 bases in his major league career, covering more than two years. The most he had ever swiped in a season was 15. Now he thought he could steal 40 in one year? People thought, just looking at the heavy, muscle-bound Canseco, that he was not much of a base stealer.

But Canseco knew that he had far more speed than most people would expect from a 230-pounder. Proud of his speed, he had run races against nearly every top sprinter in the Oakland organization. No one had ever beaten him. During his previous years in the majors, he and the Oakland coaches had concentrated on his hitting and fielding rather than worrying about his base stealing. This year would be different.

The 1988 season proved to be different for more reasons than one. The A's, who had not enjoyed a winning season since 1981, won 16 of 23 games in April. Within two weeks, they were in first place in the American League West, and they began to run away from the rest of the division. Heavyweight sluggers Dave Parker and Don Baylor, with more than 600 career home runs between them, joined McGwire and Canseco in the A's lineup. The four gave Oakland the most powerful and intimidating lineup in baseball.

Yet even among all the hitting power and the success Oakland had, it was Canseco who stood out.

With ace pitcher Bret Saberhagen on the mound, Canseco had little hope of getting his 40th home run during the game.

He nudged McGwire into a supporting role. At the All-Star game break he was well on his way to reaching his 40-40 goal. With a .290 average and a major league-leading 24 home runs, he easily won a spot in the starting lineup for the American League All-Star Team.

When the defending World Series champion Minnesota Twins closed in on the A's in midseason, baseball experts and fans wondered if Oakland would be able to maintain its hot early-season pace. Thanks to Canseco, however, Oakland kept winning. If the A's needed an important hit, Canseco usually came through.

By early September, the A's were comfortably ahead of the Twins, and Canseco was comfortably ahead of the pace he needed to crack the 40-40 mark. But Bobby Bonds had also been well ahead of pace, only to fall short. Canseco knew how easily athletes tighten up and lose their rhythm as they close in on an important mark.

With nearly three weeks to go in the season, the A's clinched their division and locked up a spot in the American League Championship Series. That left Canseco free to concentrate on his lofty goal. The A's right fielder had 39 home runs when he took the field against the Kansas City Royals on September 18. With Bret Saberhagen on the mound for the Royals, Canseco knew it would not be easy to get home run number 40.

The Royals' young right-hander, a Cy Young Award winner and World Series Most Valuable Player, had always been tough on Canseco.

In the first inning, with Luis Polonia on base, Canseco stepped to the plate to try his luck against Saberhagen. Jose ended the suspense early by whacking his 40th home run, which also drove in the deciding runs in a 3-2 victory.

The stolen bases, however, were not coming quite as easily. The baseball season wound down to the final 10 days and Canseco was still 2 short of 40. On September 23, it was his bad fortune to face left-handed pitcher Juan Nieves in a game against the Milwaukee Brewers. Because left-handers face first base during their windup, it is much more difficult for players to steal second base against them than it is against right-handers.

Before he could worry about stealing, however, Canseco had to get on base. Again he got right down to business, slapping a single off Nieves in the first inning. Taking his lead from first base, he studied Nieves as the pitcher threw to the next batter, McGwire. Having figured out the pitcher's rhythm, he dashed toward second on the next pitch. It did not look as though he was running that fast, but his long, smooth strides ate up the distance quickly. Canseco slid in ahead of the throw from catcher B.J. Surhoff for the steal. Just one to go!

Although he would have loved to have stolen the 40th base in front of the Oakland fans instead of on the road in Milwaukee, Canseco was not about to waste any chances. In the fifth inning, he laid down a bunt and beat it out. It was his first bunt single of the entire season.

As he took his lead against Nieves, Canseco's heart was pounding. "Steal, steal, steal," he thought. As Nieves wound up for his first pitch to McGwire in the inning, Canseco decided to go for it. He was so nervous, though, that his shoes stuck as if they were nailed to the ground. "My legs just froze," he said later. Instead of running toward second base, he found himself still hovering by the first base bag.

But Canseco quickly recovered his courage. On the second pitch, his legs followed orders and he barreled toward second. Again he beat Surhoff's throw. As Canseco dusted himself off, an umpire presented the base to him as a keepsake—a reminder that he had done something that no one had ever done before.

5

Texas-Sized Trade

The 1988 year-end statistics confirmed what had been obvious to anyone who had watched the Athletics play that summer: Canseco had played his best year so far. In addition to his 40-40 feat, he had lifted his batting average to .307 and cut his strikeouts to 128. Canseco led the major leagues with 42 home runs and 124 RBI. He led the American League with 120 runs scored. None of them were cheap statistics, tacked on in the late innings of games already won or lost. Of Canseco's 42 home runs, 27 had either tied the score or had given Oakland the lead. He was one of the main reasons the A's had streaked to a remarkable record of 104 wins, 58 losses.

Oakland faced the Boston Red Sox in the American League Championship Series. As had happened all year, Jose Canseco took charge. Shrugging off the taunts of the fans, Canseco broke the ice for the A's.

In the fourth inning of game one, he got just enough of a Bruce Hurst pitch to carry it over the wall and give Oakland a 1-0 lead. The A's hung on to win, 2-1.

All of Boston's hopes were pinned on game two, when Red Sox ace Roger Clemens took the mound. Clemens had won the Cy Young Award twice. The A's saw him at his best that night. Going into the seventh inning, Clemens had breezed through the Oakland lineup, striking out eight batters. With Clemens protecting a 2-0 lead, the Sox were on their way to evening up the series.

However, Dave Henderson gave the A's some hope when he stroked a single off Clemens in the seventh. That brought up Canseco. It was the key matchup of the evening: an overpowering pitcher against an overpowering batter. Clemens quickly blew two strikes past the A's slugger. Then, thinking that Henderson might steal, Clemens hurried his delivery on the third pitch. He knew as soon as he threw it that he had failed to get his usual leg kick into the pitch. It was not the kind of mistake to make around Jose Canseco. Canseco sent the pitch soaring beyond the fence to tie the game at two runs each.

That was the end of Boston's chances. Ignited by Canseco's blast, the A's rallied for a 4-3 win. The final two games were not even close. For good measure, Canseco socked a first-inning home run to help finish off Boston in game four.

That home run, his third of the play-offs, tied him with Kansas City's George Brett for the most home runs in a league championship series.

Known as the "Bash Brothers," Canseco, McGwire, Parker, and the rest of the A's confidently headed into the World Series against the Los Angeles Dodgers. Canseco lit the fuse on Oakland's World Series offensive show. Trailing 2-0 in game one, Canseco stepped to the plate with two outs and the bases loaded. After letting a pitch go by, Canseco ripped a line drive to deep center field. When it left the playing field it was still traveling with such force that it hit a television camera and put a sizeable dent in it.

Under normal circumstances, that grand slam might have propelled the A's to the title and completed Canseco's perfect season. But an improbable last-gasp, game-winning home run by the Dodgers' injury-ridden Kirk Gibson stunned the A's and broke the team's momentum. Canseco became mired in a 1 for 19 slump, and Los Angeles upset the A's, four games to one.

After the Series, however, Canseco's luck began to change. Some of the bitterness about the World Series faded on October 25 when he married Esther Haddad. Shortly thereafter, he was voted the American League's Most Valuable Player—the first unanimous choice since Reggie Jackson in 1973. And, of course he had his place in sports history as baseball's first 40-40 man.

The Dodger's Kirk Gibson (right) celebrates his game-winning home run in the bottom of the ninth inning against Oakland in game one of the 1988 World Series.

Canesco's 1989 season began poorly. He suffered an injury during spring training, and when it didn't heal he had to undergo surgery to remove part of the hamate bone in his wrist. He wasn't able to rejoin the A's until after the All-Star break in mid-July. Although loyal fans had voted him to a starting position in the All-Star game, his injury prevented him from playing. In the 65 games Canesco did play for the A's in 1989, he hit 17 home runs and had 57 RBI.

In the 1989 season, Canesco's struggles were offset by the team's success. The Oakland A's reached the highest plateau in the baseball world when they won the World Series. They swept the San Francisco Giants in four straight games. The Series that was quickly named the "Bay Bridge Series"—after the bridge that connects the cities of Oakland and San Francisco—is remembered for the strong earthquake that shook the area just before game three.

As an individual player, Canseco came back strong in 1990. He hit many more "moon shots," as one reporter called his skyward home runs, and he was crucial in helping the A's make a third straight trip to the World Series. Although Canseco seemed to be back on track, the A's lost the Series to the Cincinnati Reds.

The A's slipped from first place in the division standings in 1991. But again Canseco's performance was impressive. On August 19, he hit his 200th home run. The 40-40 man reached this goal in only 3,067 at bats. Only nine players in baseball history had hit 200 homers in fewer at bats. His 44 home runs of the season tied him with Detroit's Cecil Fielder for the American League home-run title.

In 1992, however, Jose Canseco's whole life changed. The Oakland A's were leading by 7½ games in the American League West, and they were on their way to another division title. On August 31, the A's were at home in the Oakland-Alameda Coliseum facing the Baltimore Orioles. In the bottom of the first inning, Canseco was in the on-deck circle preparing to bat. Tony La Russa suddenly called him back to the dugout

Canseco at bat for his new team, the Texas Rangers, after being part of the biggest baseball trade in 1992

and told him he had been traded to the Texas Rangers.

Considering his past performance, Canseco's 1992 season had not been going well. His back was bothering him and his shoulder was constantly sore. At the time of the trade, he was hitting .246 with 22 home runs, and 72 RBI. Even so, Canseco could not disguise his disappointment at the turn of events. "I'm hurt. I'm not a robot," he protested. Canseco had spent his ten-year professional baseball career with Oakland, and his contract was good for three more years. Needless to say, both the baseball world and Jose Canseco were shocked by the trade. "I don't know what really happened. Maybe I'll never know the reason I was traded," he said.

The trade took place just two hours before teams would no longer be able to make trades for the rest of the season. Even La Russa and the Texas manager Tom Grieve seemed surprised by the trade. Yet both teams had something the other wanted. The Oakland A's wanted to strengthen their team's pitching staff. The Texas Rangers could not pass up the opportunity to acquire a big-name player like Jose Canseco, with his powerful swing and the pop-star quality he brought to the game.

The trade wasn't the only thing disrupting Canseco's life. His personal life was also filled with disappointments. After four years of marriage, Esther and Jose filed for divorce in November. Hurricane Andrew destroyed Canseco's home in Biscayne Bay, Florida. His debut as a Texas Ranger did not go well either. He went 0-4, striking out twice.

Despite the upheaval and disappointment brought by 1992, Canseco is optimistic about his future in baseball. He promised the Rangers great things for 1993, saying "Now I will have a chance to get my health back. I'll work hard in the offseason. I'll come back 100 percent."

JOSE CANSECO'S BASEBALL STATISTICS

Minor Leagues

Year	Club (class)	Games	At Bats	Runs	Hits	Home Runs	RBI	Batting Average	Strike-outs	Stolen Bases
1982	Miami (A)	6	9	0	1	0	0	.111	3	0
1982	Idaho Falls (A)	28	57	13	15	2	7	.263	13	3
1983	Madison (A)	34	88	8	14	3	10	.159	36	2
1983	Medford (A)	59	197	34	53	11	40	.269	78	6
1984	Modesto (A)	116	410	61	113	15	73	.276	127	10
1985	Huntsville (AA)	58	211	47	67	25	80	.318	55	6
1985	Tacoma (AAA)	60	233	41	81	11	47	.348	66	5
Minor League Totals		361	1,205	204	344	67	257	.286	378	32

Minor League Highlight:

Southern League Most Valuable Player, 1985.

Major Leagues

Year	Club	Games	At Bats	Runs	Hits	Home Runs	RBI	Batting Average	Strike-outs	Stolen Bases
1985	Oakland	29	96	16	29	5	13	.302	31	1
1986	Oakland	157	600	85	144	33	117	.240	175	15
1987	Oakland	159	630	81	162	31	113	.257	157	15
1988	Oakland	158	610	120	187	42	124	.307	128	40
1989	Oakland	65	227	40	61	17	57	.269	69	6
1990	Oakland	131	481	83	132	37	101	.274	158	19
1991	Oakland	154	572	115	152	44	122	.266	152	26
1992	Oakland-Texas	119	439	74	107	26	87	.244	128	3
Major League Totals (regular season)		972	3,655	614	974	235	734	.266	998	125

Major League Highlights:

American League Most Valuable Player, 1988.
American League All-Star Team, 1986, 1988, 1989, 1990, 1991, 1992.
American League Rookie of the Year, 1986.

ACKNOWLEDGMENTS

Photographs are reproduced through the permission of: Oakland A's, pp. 6, 10, 56; Mark Levine/SportsChrome East/West, p. 9; Coral Park High School (Miami), pp. 14, 17; Baseball Card Trading Post, pp. 12, 29; Brian Drake/SportsChrome East/West, pp. 19, 33; Mitchell B. Reibel/SportsChrome East/West, pp. 20, 24, 33, 36, 41, 49; California Angels, p. 26; Texas Rangers, pp. 1, 2, 53; Dennis Desprois/San Francisco Giants, p. 38; Cincinnati Reds, p. 39; Kansas City Royals, p. 42; John McDermott/SportsChrome East/West, p. 46; Los Angeles Dodgers, p. 51.

Front and back cover photographs are courtesy of the Texas Rangers.